Editor's Choice for the 2001 Transcontinental Poetry Award

A Commerce of Moments

Sofia M. Starnes

Pavement Saw Press
Ohio   2003

Acknowledgments: Grateful acknowledgment is made to the publications in which these poems first appeared: Calapooya, Defined Providence, Folio, Gulf Coast, Hayden's Ferry Review, Hubbub, Nightsun, Pavement Saw, Pleiades, Poet Lore, The Laurel Review, The Lucid Stone, The MacGuffin, The Marlboro Review, Sow's Ear Poetry Review, Turnings.

My gratitude as well to the Aldrich Museum of Contemporary Art for publication of *The Soul's Landscape*, a chapbook in which several poems of this collection were published. Also, warmest personal thanks to photographic artist Kathy Sturgeon, whose work inspired a significant number of these poems.

Editor: David Baratier
Associate Editor: Stephen Mainard
Cover Photo (Old Manila): W. H. Starnes, Jr.

Pavement Saw Press
PO Box 6291
Columbus, OH 43206
pavementsaw.org

Ohio Arts Council
A STATE AGENCY
THAT SUPPORTS PUBLIC
PROGRAMS IN THE ARTS

Products are available through the publisher or through:
SPD / 1341 Seventh St. / Berkeley, CA 94710 / 800.869.7553

Editor's Choice for the 2001 Transcontinental Poetry Award for an outstanding first book-length collection of poetry or prose. We read yearly from June 1st until August 15th. Send an SASE for details.

CONTENTS

The Stakes

The Pilgrim's Shadows
Apples
Shadows of Innocence
Similes
The Doorway
The Previous Hour
The Tightrope
The Shape of Ancestry
Garlic
The Procession
Witching Cloths
The Soul's Landscape
Nuptials
A Ritual of Flight
Rituals of Repentance
Journey Bird
Viernes Santo
Ave Maria

The Commerce

A Name for God

The Prize

Behold the Body
Banígs
Lola's Window
The Shadow in the Attic
Coat
Threshold
Our Impatient Ones
The Limp
The Long Life
The Body's Hope
Flores de Mayo
Delirium
Beloved
Absolution
The Diagnosis
My Father's House
One Sweet Invincible
Nunc Dimitis

For Menci, Pili, Chaco and Tere
Habemus ad Dominum

and

For Bill
Pondus meum amor meus

THE STAKES

THE PILGRIM'S SHADOWS

Bonelight: unlike our other torches, it makes
        the fine wood spindle on our terrace

blood-kin of the tibia, and the round rosette
        on the banister, the youngest child

of bone, for whom we burn the homelight
        on the porch. Our eyes weary

of the same angular glee, vee-shaped happiness
        on lips as they have always been,

and of the simper which can be no other.
        And so, we leave.

Ah, there is something to be said for aging,
        for the idle giving in to gray

which makes for daily discoveries,
        for the newness of this earnest

face, thinning, thinning slowly, and
        for the changeful notches on those

whom we have loved so differently.
        With our backs to the familiar

flood-beam on the eave, where the driveway
        is mere elbow, and a willow nods

its sheep-head in fake sleep, we signify
        our shadows in this bonelight, as

Narcissus would, in truth unmindful of our fairness,
        which must differ, or of the clear

precision of our jaw, for that, too, shifts, or
    of the widowed wishbone

unwished this way and that...
    We are drawn only by this assurance:

this shadow-region is ourself, in quiet company
    with every street-lamp, door-light,

slim, peculiar flash-bulb — short-lived.

APPLES

Out of a hilltop burning, this call:
> *Of the tree of life, you shall not eat;*

the rest is bounty.
>   He might have said: out of the common

bone, you shall not pick, you shall not scratch
>   the ground for roots, for you have none; rest

with your eyes east-borne, close them to the red
>   fire seeding your backs,

while you love. You shall not laugh louder than
>   the towhee laughs in your second of joy;

you shall not feed its fledgling with your thistle.
>   Oh, and forget the lion and its cub,

the weasel and its pup, the hare's fruitfulness.
>   Do not chase them past the honeysuckle...

>   He might have ended
our excess, and left us with too sweet a knowing,

>   but he said: *Of the tree of life, you shall not eat;*
the rest is bounty.

We take forever with the setting of each meal.
>   Every lettuce head comes wrapped in clear

plastic, the neatest knot, and the leeks, three
>   in a bunch, with vein-like rubber girding.

The same goes, over and over, for the green
>   flowerets in square parcels, the blackberries

double-tiered in a tray, the late-born
      apples in their beds, their smooth globes,

seductive. Obsessed, we count them: this
      much for us, this for the children, for Mamá…

After the meal, we hunger for the tree,
      for its knowing of a new world — unlike us,

      the way it sweetens the unfed.

Shadows of Innocence

Purewhite, paperwhites,
odor of petals on the wicker-stand on which

we lean.
Deathwhite, dogwood white, hybrid

shadows behind the screened porch...
We have been cautioned not

to invade the white square off the house,
where the dead live.

          Why did you bring the bulbs
indoors this year?   Fresh spring-

whites are for old slabs with their prone angels.
Remember the dotted hearts in our earliest

missals, their venial lesson, scent
of onion skin. We learned

from them never to flirt with a fragrance,
for the sake of our faithfulness.

          Blameless lily-white,
how it escapes us, as white always does,

with the merest gesture: a finger
smudge on the slick envelope, thin trickle

on the swab where a nail
ripped, velvet eye-shade against the tissue,

powdery death.
Remember the white cassock our priest wore

in summer heat, like a returning *santo*?
           It dropped its length on stubby

feet, into our muddy garden.

SIMILES

This day, you will be with me...

Out of our old porch-nights —
the white of chairs in an empty portico, vague

against the vinyl, the heel-born patter
on flagstones in the walk, a skillet

lilting off a second skillet in the black throat
of the cupboard.

Out of our old door-dust —
the day's rum cake, brown-flecked

as a girl's knees in summer, the night-
specks, fretful as first lipstick, and as gone.

We hear the low squeaks in slow hinges;
the final flap-flap of skirts well into the quiet.

And we say: the young return, just like
the moon returns, midnight matter we watch

as we watched babies out of sonograms,
waxing closer, closely into birth;

the dead will rise, because the oak
verbs out of its acorn with hardly a hush,

inevitably; and ancients
will sweeten our loss, the way loose wings

sweeten the hidden comb, after a spring's
excursion.

Yet all this is nothing but an artifact,
a schedule laid out for a trip nowhere near

taken: half-breath out of a mint melting,
half-sky pinched between rows at an ascent.

                              Remember me,
the good thief said, himself, remembering.

And he leaned over, blood
through boldness, to figure out where —

for Christ's sake — his wish hung.
This once, not simile or trick: his dawn,

a heartache.

The Doorway

The door slipped a ribbon of April under-
foot, where Mamá stood,

where the child was no longer dust in the teak
box, but bright

knob of reference, nagging windsong of a crack,
wood shavings.

And the aroma of closed crib, like sweet
pine bark, scented

her yard's crocus.
    Spring comes as a season ajar,

with access to both spaces,
balconies from which we look. There, coaxed into

and out of living, we must number
and draw, juggle toys, work out puzzles to define

abide: anticipate, expect, limp out of longing.
Near us, hinges burn with light

on their backbones,
and the door hums.

    Saffron blooms for two weeks
in the fall. We know the soil before it,

the soil after it, the small wound on which its purple
clumps, withers. The flower leaves

a subdued scar
for the next blossom.

Ah, the door swings fully
in November, and the child, dusty and delivered,

climbs over the rail.
His small hands scoop and love, nothing more.

for Antoñito

THE PREVIOUS HOUR

Mud on the brown back
of the carabao, mud

on its ropelike tail,
complacently determining

the hour. Afternoon.
The heat drew ribbons

on the slopes, roads
we rode on with our eyes —

Is this all we will ever see?
        Our previous hour,

deprived of knowing how
the sweat would dry up

into clouds, and the dense
scent of our weariness

would turn into a languor
of bone lotus on the bed,

how the night we wore
diluted on our backs, damp

cotton clinging, the mat
leaving square nibbles

on our cheeks, would become
next hour of blank light,

amnesiac hour, never once
recalling what the body

and soul foresaw —
      that afternoon of mud

shells, hide of blistered arches,
a full sun curdling, setting

on its humps.

THE TIGHTROPE

Mid-summer: a certain temptation
to settle here, before the final

leg of the journey, when the year teeters like an acrobat
in white tights

over a plaza's netting.
(Days and devils labor inches apart...)

Let's say we, too, attempt our balance on two stilts,
bone-thin,

with no other crutch,
the way the obsessive artist of August fiestas leaned

on twin álamos for his evenness.
When he built his home, he hollowed double hearths

and a blind threshold to match the east-wing door;
in the silent plot behind the house,

he planted a double ligament of liana
toward a second tomb.

Always in pure duality —
Let's say we leave out every thirdness, the odd drone

hovering over a bee-line, the loose tongue
in the uncommon serpent,

threading a twig... instead,
we slip into a commerce of moments: one-two,

one-two: noon gossip for midnight truth,
leaf-lethargy for home.

Two crows have scared the crickets balancing our luck —
a caw, a pull,

a pause —
what could, what must become of a life.

THE SHAPE OF ANCESTRY

Candlelight: nothing
but a father's fingers closing in

on the flame; thumb and index pitch
toward it, shutter-tight;

he winks, re-stages the invasion for his children,
wildfire

which will not burn.
A black film caps his digits, full-blown

negative bequeathing some old photograph.
                    He never nudges the flare,

broad canna in true observance of bloom;
instead, he teases it,

angles the glow gregarious, half-mesmerizing
himself.

The white wax drips,
drips with latter-leaf patience, the wick fizzles

downhill to its sconce,
                    as if in chase of the dying.

Now you have seen how
our ancestors vanish around us, how

they become white pastures, cold land masses
amid which we blaze.   At length,

our portions join them.
After the wick wizens, the father melts the wax

into a new body,
wide-ribbed, faithfully rotund. He pauses,

and the flesh solidifies, no longer venturesome.
Once more, a flame jitters back,

child out of the rubble.

GARLIC

Come, peel away its shape
and scent, sheaths that wrinkle clove with clove,

come tightly to the wishful nibs.
How they last...

Here, in a blue, ancestral store
with blue plates, blue flowers, cobalt jars with fine brass

necks, blue billows,
here, the old *abuelos* breathe. Their dry

air dances up and under beams where garlic hangs
in *ristras*. This was their word

for garlic-string; no other sound as restless or as risible —
Listen hard: *ris-s-s-tra*... perfect lips for bulbs

with hidden laughter.
Ah, no one knows how our ancestors chuckled,

their bequeathing sedate, still-life brushed
of all afternoon grin.

> *Leave it here to be giggled in time,*
> *leave the joke of the colonel, bugle-call to eclipse,*
> *leave the blunder of puns fathers dream up.*

Now, the garlic, wry and
unblundering, has shrunk to munificent smell,

like the old men.
Whether beaten or bundled to rest, at the end their spiced

faces sprang open and laughed: at the ironic,
at the inert spun to quickness, at the sight of this summer

and that, and the next, mulled in love, without sweat,
into everness. Never mind

that their morsels come stark and unmixed.
Let us pluck them, allot them unhurried — sniff and slice

of their luck.
Breathe, posterity, breathe their aroma commingling

with oil and with broth... blue
my gene, blue my odorous bowl where they laugh.

THE PROCESSION

They have shaped their absence for us
            at the gate, some as heel-

marks where the garden cleared, transferring
            its want; they have laid

the stones afresh in telltale slant, loose
            under our feet; and the rest,

the best of them, have borne their own saints
            on their columns, farther in,

where the birds live.
            We, the doubtful, the miscarried,

wrestle back —
            In the night, the shadows tighten,

heel to thumbmark,
            into buttonhole of birth; after that,

the flagstones stumble into place
            for the late-comers; and at mid-

night (how we watch them!), all those
            humped bearers of saints bear

the columns out of sight, feed their luminous
            grackles... Hence we wonder where

they go and whom they meet at the garden's
            annulment; what they whisper,

when they notice (if they do, from their
            abandon), the soft buttonhole

of absence in our bodies, the loose stone
            lodged in the smallness of our backs;

and in moonlight, the saint's
            ribcage, scrubbed clean of its zeal,

bracing our lost ardor.

WITCHING CLOTHS

That night we did not question stars,
        or from what milk-white

mother they would dribble to our chins,
        why they blinked,

while we who were younger and human,
        sulked in shut-eye greyness

under sheets.
        Mamá was going to a dance.

She wore blackness: not a black *mantilla*
        or a black skirt, but blackness

in a swirl, and she opened up her shelter
        to our hands, heads, hair that

quieted under the airless tent: right, left, right,
        left, around her stockinged legs…

        Niñas, niñas, we'll be late.

Ah, she had a rare laugh, not one to heed
        but to contemplate in privacy,

as you would a full moon on a blue month,
        to mirror in. That night

it escaped the black bluff, cool and mossy,
        her endangered cave —

(Push, push away the shifting folds, no longer
        dear without a view of her.)

                    And we learned
we could be this, expectant but at war beyond

her eyes, in the manner of the old
                    photographer: the witching

cloth, the lantern, loud and livid,
                    vanishing, the explosive cold.

But a soul learned otherwise:
                    that it could not behold itself

in place, in darkness.

THE SOUL'S LANDSCAPE

Ah, what the soul gives for shape —
           to be handled head-first

at the temple, to be cumbered
           with cotton, white puffs

from plantations in heat; what it gives
           for the flick, flick elastic

on wrists, loose-leaf palms it befriends,
           at its youngest — for the sake

of all this, and this place.
           Love me now with your

hands (says the soul, half-exploring its
           landscape), better me

with embodiment; come, angle the ribs
           where they beach into

longing; come, finger the oval description
           of death, smallest hope

for cessation. When the room is redundant
           of space, and its walls

wish for closure, thumb my corners
           up, inward, wade your lips

through the ridge where they meet,
           to allow recollection.

I must love with the tissue and the gloss
           that embody: cellule, elegy,

ghost, danger, languish... all those words
                out of context for souls,

god-forsaken, whiplash of the neck —
                           Interim

is the word I would use the most cautiously;
                how precarious its hum,

ear to earth, plumbing earth, earthwise.

NUPTIALS

Let us keep this
between us, my love:
sacred narrow, *arroyo*

where humbly
the excesses prove
earthwise their worth,

the whole process,
a manner of rendering
rain unto rain, for the next

thirst. Chaste exchange
at its ripest, slightly
different this from

the snake's —
Have you noticed?
She must squeeze her own

gold out of perilous peel,
while we stay
with the death clinging

whole on our skin when
it storms, or whenever
we dip in the bath, plunge

our feet in the coldest
of springs. And the waters
gleam there, never

seeping their way into us.
We have other desires...
How we drink

from the earthenware
ewer of lips, how we press
our hope tightly to keep

that one adamant blessing
inside, rightly homed,
rightly braved. Sweet

benevolent host:
where we embrace, there
we give up abundance.

A RITUAL OF FLIGHT

Zoar is where we'll settle next, Lot said, and God
agreed, for he had lost his wager,

his town snapping in heat's holiness, shock
after shock of houses, wood

barns, the erratic loft burnt under unloving.
There were no sinless few,

not fifty, or forty-five, or forty, or even ten
white souls to whitewash

patios, plant their milky azaleas in yards of goodness.
                    I love them all, God said,

I would have saved them all, but I myself
am bound within the chosen,

that pool of godly genes flaring their heads, their hearts
hotter than all others,

willow and fireweed from allocated ash.
Today we shudder at these: chicory

clumps, roaches in far nests of old credenzas, egg to egg,
malignant cells that flower at close range, dark

to darkness cloned in sacred corpses.
We watch their passing as innocents: *surely we are not*

one of them, not one in the cold crowd, the mass grave
where a fine rose pops open, all by itself.

Don't, don't look back.
There is no way to tell where the blaze stops, or if

our skirts have scalloped into flames;
we cannot halo out the fireline with our toes,

or sanctify our luck.
                    Between our wagers (odds

against kindle, odds against ash) we wonder why
heat tantalized Lot's wife,

and why she looked.
                    The salt of tears — was it? Was she

so terrified she might be God's?

RITUALS OF REPENTANCE

Come, make me medieval,
night-heat breaking temperate truce

on the pulpit.
Let me clamor *atone,*

somber song of the tonsured,
the sack-clothed, the beggar who limped

and laid siege with half-eye, half-illusion.
Let me write of *thee* lovers, *thee*

seekers, *thee...*

          Our bodies remain
       pre-millenial

       with the rose of renewal fast-folding,
       faces blue round the ears where we hear

       the cold warnings:
       At the waters,

       repent; at the cumulus rant on your window,
       repent; at the angry applause of a floodgate,

       come inside, waive the gold-rush with
       no resurrection; repent.

       Unafraid, we are born into different dread.

    Hush, dear body, it's over.
The hell-chatter, the devil-

beast crawling, caressing the stone
in your ribs. Press a hand to the thud-thud,

the erratic or solemnly paused heart;
love it back into normalcy.

We must grow antibodies
and flowers immune to new deaths,

never theirs, toss their nosegays out,
serve fresh meats with nasturtiums;

we are ours, only ours to pump heart,
our penances fertile now, summers now,

mushrooming large...

JOURNEY BIRD

com'om che torna a la perduta strada,
che 'nfino ad essa li pare ire in vano.*
                                    Dante Alighieri. **Purgatorio.**

Dustwalk: We shake the grit off our feet, off
        the blonde sneakers, combed hem of our jeans,

threading home, with no remembrance
        of the driveways we drove up earlier today,

out of duty. Out of duty, too, we forget the loved
        ones tucked into back yards. Doubling over,

they hummock like sedum mounds, green hearts
        pumping a late hope.

Think about it. The moment we come home, we
        who have eyes over our shoulder must shut

them, shutter out old faces, vigils on wayside
        fences, where they drew back unkissed.

We call forgetfulness the dying
        of the journey bird, which we leave alone.

We have no extra afternoons for burials.
        When the brick appears local at last,

we recognize the young myrtle, feasting on its beetles
        (or is it otherwise?), its pregnancy plowing

inward, caress-full. And the orgy will prove fatal
        for the bloom. But we forget this, too — up

the walk, up the placid porch between rows
        of newfound geraniums, up to the front door

we left open. Right there, every motion
        comes back to us, where the shaft of a repeated

morning bleaches the knob, forces
        remembrance out of white metal: white knee-

caps, white nape under the white dogwood,
        stare of the white eye, white locks on the night-

hawk, loosening.
        Memory keeps us passengers still, dust-born.

like one returning to a lost pathway
who, till he finds it, seems to move in vain. (Trans. Allen Mendelbaum)

VIERNES SANTO

Black cowls, and the scuffle of bare
        feet, occasionally a chain clacks

against the pavement, snags
        a cellophane wrapper, sweet-bled;

it drags this minor sin with all the others.
        This is Good Friday in Sevilla.

A man chants a *saeta*, to become
        the moment's cock. He crows twice,

neck stretched, riddling the hustle of feet.
        It has been said:

from all creation, one creature sings after denial.
        They bear the Christ first —

The float's skirt drapes over fifty men,
        whose swollen soles throb further.

Cyrenaic, this giant centipede
        claws uphill to the thump-thump

of a stick. Now comes a second square
        of penitents, frayed at the edges, where

children dangle like loose threads.
        (Not the children, we say;

they have not sinned.)
        Their fathers sway behind them: *un, dos,*

un, dos, dancing their *Virgen*
        under a sea-way of lights. She will not

contemplate her son, if they can help it.
      For this, the wavelength of wicks, squall

of voices, a *viva*
      that chars the air to the cathedral.

All this exists, but we, late-born
      mestizos, cannot possess it—-

Our blood is out of sight. Step-hold the night;
      we step-hold atonement.

AVE MARIA

Scent of sweet
impatience, the melon
husk holds August

in its pulp;
>   *Hail Mary*
>   *full of grace.*

The summer sores,
once close to festering,
now flower thickly,

freely where they
wept; the grove and
graveyard bear

similar swells.
Full are the tombs,
fuller the womb,

the ovum opening
to strange gust
in the middle of its

breath.
We fail
to understand,
>   *Hail Mary,*
>   *Mother of God.*

All we recall
is ripeness, long
awaited in the stalls,

plum, peach,
or apricot still firm
against our thumb.
>Pray, pray for us
>now and in the
>hour

Wait, it is not yet
time.

THE COMMERCE

conscience: a knowing with

Nahum, prophet, 7th century B.C., Crispine, martyr in Tunisia, 4th century; Sabbas, abbot from Cappadocia, founder of the laura (monastery) of Mar Saba in Judea, 5th-6th centuries; Eulalia and Julia, martyrs, Merida, Spain, 5th century; Nimatullah Youssef, priest in Hardin, Lebanon, 19th century; Judicael, king, Brittany, 6th-7th centuries; Thorlak, bishop, Iceland, 12th century; Adelaide, empress, Germany, 10th century; Elizabeth Rose, abbess at the monastery of Chelles, France, 12th century.

A NAME FOR GOD

> *Does anyone have the foggiest idea what sort of power we*
> *so blithely invoke?*
> Annie Dillard: **Teaching a Stone to Talk**

I

The disconcert of time, the unharmony of air
       that homes deathward, no more desirous of this

domicile than its lung, the smallness of a lull
       between two apartments, where a vacancy lags:

out of these, our day-worn, night-intimation
       of a god. We have come, oh, hardly closer

than a darkroom's inkling of red-eyes, blonde
       hair flashed and weary, the candid joy of being

almost immortal on a couch, with the rest,
       our hopeful ones. At length, a snapshot, square

and solid, will un-doubt us.

~~~

II

Up, down the entrails of the house; up, down
      the basement stairs, the attic ladder whose loose

dovetail dances on the third step... Underfoot,
      among rungs, comes the smell of a buffeted

summer, of beleaguered magnolias unearthing
      their breath, white and wet, of the grease in a back-

hoe scheming the lot, of the pulleys with mud purled
      around them. Foul to fragrant they shift, taproot

blood and the odor of hands, culled and common,
      resetting a frontage of ribs. Thus, like pestering

hounds, with our noses we know of the copse,
      of the succulent season, of men prior to drywalls,

breaking ground. On the scaffolds, a pigeon erupts,
      tufts apart, almost scentless as God.

~~~

III

Bless the foggy notion, the ages-long surplice
     which keeps God at length. Bless the green

coats of ushers, the neat and elaborate letters
     they hand out, the byline of priests; bless

the blue window costume, the Mother perched
     high: her stone lamb, her stone stalk, the stone's

insufficience... Bless (forgive me for this)
     the immaculate bread, the sweet wine with

exquisite taste which, in kindness, conceals.
     Ours alone, tipsy, tender, this banquet-like

masque, hunch of bliss, heart of saneness which
     misses (thank heavens) the heave, heavy hand

of an earthquake, the come-near of God.
     Bless, oh, bless the grotesque, the mollified

master humped holy, the backload of stars.

~~~

IV

Pater noster, qui es in caelis:
sanctificetur nomen tuum…

Tribe-borne, a father-name, its out-growth
    obvious when we sang ringbird in the yard,

and wiped our fingers clean against the denim,
    which made us "it" or "innocent."

Outdoors, chased and chasers, rare and rank,
    we were all siblings.

Tribe-raised, we could not be content to know
    God as first-birth of countless creatures, bone

out of whose abundant bones the question rises:
    Is there no private game to engage a god in,

certain shared and sharing, thumb against thumb,
    one-to-one-child play, far from leaves

on leaves on leaves in dense plantation?
    We kiss one face after another in our tribe,

to enamor a god, we wrinkle everness between lips:
    the weak blessed, the rough blessed, the wet

linen against all chins blessed.
    Ah, despite our tremor at heart-holding,

at the pressure which finds the skin scabbed
    and unable to race from immediate to intimate,

    we make love...

~~~

V

Light to light, there is only con-*science*,
       a crystal-clear view of a place, with all others.

Hear Nahum: God is good; kiss the head
       of Crispine in the block, ripe as pomegranate,

fuller of seed; slip away with Sabbas, laura-homed,
       gold-oasised; take Eulalia and Julia uphill,

with their grapes unconsumed, safe at last
       in Mar Saba. (We are free from the sniper

who fires without ancients or ash.)
       Hear God call: Nimatullah Youssef, Judicael,

Thorlak, Adelaide, Elizabeth Rose... They've
       become summer fruit in our flesh, bodied-sweet.

Then God's voice comes, entire as the willow's fore-
       warning of winds, its rushed ruffling of hair.

And God hums. Hear him clearing his throat,
       like the intricate lover who calls and acquaints

his remembrance to the shape of her name:
       all exhaustive, each night, yet all-mutual. After

love, they soft-speak back and forth, hope and
       hollow. Thus, divine and beloved break silence:

in heart-home, heart desire, out of heartsore.

~~~

THE PRIZE

BEHOLD THE BODY

A certain distance to behold how
        the leg angles from its torso, where

the long thigh separates from the sweet
        cave, exactly; half-an-inch nearer,

and the hip would haze itself,
        like a morning that is never quite

morning when it drizzles. We squint
        to bring the ridgelines into focus.

It may be wiser to lean back, the way
        the abelia eases farther on its fine

elbows to view the house from the right
        hillock: the house ells away behind

frostbitten hollies, goose-neck leaves
        creeping outward from its black under.

This must be how the Godhead
        watches us, how the brilliant spine

arches toward us,
        but never too close, to avoid the costly

overlap. Day and night, the Good hand
        wheedles us, back-tugging our loose

hair, invisible.
        And we voice our loudest complaint ever:

Come out now, where we can see you...
        and we forget to blink.

After dark,
I settle into your nestful collar-bones, like

the burrower with extinct eyes, figuring
        its burrow from its fur. Always your hand,

the *good* hand, teases my head back;
        your fingers river it with their pebbly

knuckles —
        and the ear heeds your bated splash,

splash like no other.
        Thus may we behold our bodies sloping

farther into sight,
        worship their delicate light-forms.

BANÍGS

Bless the lure of the closet;
bless the ancients who bundled their beds,

tucked the giveaway pleats, plaits
of grass where they wish-

wore their sheen, and their spines curved.
(Ah, the mornings

were separate then from those issues
of sleep.)

      Bless the floors, lightwashed, empty,
where the espousals took place —

unattended
by early well-wishers.

Hours later, the guests ambled in, round
and round in their naiveté,

their eyes blind to the unnatural light
in the wood boards, the oils

settling the cracks.
Overflowing, they tasted desire for this

spot, worshipped on, worshipped traceless.
           At Communion some

Sundays, a little wine spills, kiss exposed
on the marble. And we dab it

distressed, at the stress of old genes, soak
its fruit with a small purifier,

like the linen that wraps a desire:
>*hide it whole,*
>*hide it holy.*

Hence is love partly secret,
an evening of grass, cross-abrading of leaves

on our bodies, when we rise.

banigs: woven leaf mats, traditional Philippine bedding.

LOLA'S WINDOW

The call to make-believe, later forbidden,
a liturgy of ghosts —

      Every night she settled near
the window, rosary and wrinkle on the wood.

The moon dimpled to zero on her lap, remade
eclipse, harelip of a sun's invasion.

And in that shade, cool and somnolent,
her memory grew certain.

      Once she was a child in a resplendent
room, hoping for an annunciation —

drive of wings down and inward,
ballet in the weave of a blind. There she'd hear

an angel's liquid claim, salt-sweet treasure —
      Come where the brilliance is yours.
      Come, carry off the cry.

Released at last of all painstaking
growth, of hands out of jackstones and sipa,

out of the box-like patintero she could not play,
not being swift enough.

Only the god of the white room.
      This you do and only this
      for your patio of light.

Midnight dropped its pearl under her eaves,
nugget of those years when the moon

always reached, always rescued.
      Loss is an old but ample word for ghost; prize
      is the better word for angel.

sipa, patintero: children's games in Manila.

THE SHADOW IN THE ATTIC

            Dry dust and remembrance
in the rafters: the roof wheezes grey air,

a squirrel fuzzes its fur against
the grille; the sun patches hunchback covers,

blanches my feet.
                        Ropablanca,

the women would say, scurrying
their children...   And the coalman (night

hood and star eye) would shore his hands
inward, fair inlets he pulled undersea,

false reefs and true rivers, mistakes of mimosas
repetalled with cells, all that dead

skin our skin could have blessed by caressing.
Now, the roof and the sun, trick

and trapdoor, restore him in shafts, blonde
hatch where I meet the foregone when it rains,

when the fan snaps its belt in mid-
summer, or the circuitry crackles in need —

and the attic rasps, rasps:
            Climb up to this room where he hides.

How the man slipped away, his immaculate
markings still frazzling the coal,

how he stretched into dismal, disarming
the heated box-heart —   ah, that memory's

fright, how it sits in the room with its regret,
somber.

Ropablanca: old colloquial Spanish term for the skin ailment known as vitiligo.

COAT

More than a loss of habit,
when we hang the jacket on its peg —

the invertebrate off us and wanting, variable
caress we leave behind.

It reminds us of those loose shifts we were bused
to, crew-necked and scarfed: daytime, grave-

yard, the dangling noon hour brightly dressed.
Not one of them would cling to us

becoming.
Someone left a coat in the hall closet years ago,

but we never learned who, or why he never
missed it. Like an espalier stitched

onto the wrong wall, it limped into a leafless
motif, mystified.

                    Every garment hangs
on our backbones as metaphor, bundling the body's

hope. Every houndstooth sweater and split-skirt
becomes torso and thigh, when thus needed,

to fasten a god's summer-membered anatomy.
And this god, wordful or unwording,

grave or capriciously garbed,
rivers into and out of our wear:

waterproofs, winter gloves, loose capotes we leave
unattended, where the sun will not reach

or re-dress. Still, the jacket undresses its loss
in the way of the no-soul, the no-god...

and we escape, with our body as wrap — terrified
lest we drop strips of clothing.

THRESHOLD

The night retrieves its blackness from our tight-lipped
mouths, when

hesitant we lock our legs together,
hug our knees, our forefinger and thumb pressed

against each other, unyielding.
There is no lack of secret places in our bodies,

hermit rooms with their own doubt: if not lucency,
then what? Somber faces

from the blind eye of the moon,
women in translucent gauze, hustling through their veils,

men who weep and wipe the ache
with the backside of their hands,

naked children, washed clean with the hose,
after a good cry. All these: brim

and basin in the corners of closed
lips, in breaths we taste and recognize as theirs

whom we forgot.
                    Ah, the light-cry quickened

out of child, the first communion veil, all snow, all god,
the confirmation fingers posying our cheeks —

innocence that gravitates, recurring night-
like in the far reach of our mouths, nightlike in tethered

thighs anxious at their giving.
                 And so the body prays: Come

through the light-sore threshold of my hands,
into my threadlike hallways. Come

through the nibble of lost things; come,
prize the morning of my whole flesh open.

OUR IMPATIENT ONES

Spring-worthy is the poem that hollows out a nest
between two words,

and leaves us with the recondite impatience
of a buttonhole left vacant,

or of the neckline wavering behind the nape,
slightly lower than we're told

would be acceptable.
Soft-spoken but imperative, our want weeps open

in a vee, as in the unguarded
valley of a *terno's* back, where the silkworm

warps its string of invitation, and the powdered skin
dimples its disguise.

What else are we to seek?
A novel way of tonguing forth spring-bones

in resurrection, a novel way to make us
understood. Our blouses river painfully in front,

visible as the empty tombs we'll watch in
fascination at our death.

Oh, how the *gumamela* rouges, dies
at its crimsonest, how the glue-trapped salamander

shivers every black cord in display,
for its salvation... how the endangered serpent

arches, tempted before tempting,
between clumps of evergreen.

We know at last what everyone is wanting —
their fingers shuttle, love to flaw, flotsam to love.

And the dead rib, past its anguish, rises...

terno: Philippine woman's dress
gumamela: Philippine flower.

The Limp

Between *posada* and *posada*,
              we limp sideways,

graceless in our unknowing.
              We should have

watched where the lamb strayed,
              listened to the creak,

creak of the sheepgate, portent
              of our bedroom door.

We tossed our sheets too promptly,
              the moonface

dropped its loneliness, cheek-first
              on the pillow;

and the soul nuzzled back: *I will*
              bind my left foot to your right...

Some nights the body sleeps
              at the foot of the bed.

(Are you shocked?) It snores,
              purrs, reminds us

of an opossum on the road,
              for whom we swerve

or not; either way, something
              is forever changed:

the thrush we would have blinded
              with our headlamps

twitches right, our tiremarks
                    open riddles out of rain,

a naysay-yeasay river
                    for the next car. Because

of this, they (not we)
                    have splattered mud

against fair ankles, long-
                    limbed, iridescent

pedestrian. (Hence will her shadow
                    haunt us.)

Ah, wake up, my kind beloved
                    body —

with our limp we tip the fickle balance.

THE LONG LIFE

The body learns this from the cold:
a vagueness of shape, mists so moth-like they never

sit still — wing-lobe fine, while they flutter.
In the cold, windows ice

into pupas with the rarest unease, like a bug's
aneurism, eruptive.

                    Come to freeze,
between mating and birth; gone to haze.

We were born without this,
under copious bananas which ripened inside us,

unseen. And we leafed out,
complacent, sweet on time and on always.

                    A distracted hibiscus once
doubled its blooms, double-dared the bee's urge,

content that a wind, brush-blown, thick,
would carry its seed March through March.

I suppose its old redness still burns
(now, a blush, now, a death), in view of that porch,

where we learned how good life was,
prolonged.

Out of cold things, the backbone discovers its jolt,
start of frost, hornet-waist

tight, its closure of summer.
                    There is only this hour

for a thought to become
the word's plenty, for the body to clear out of fog,

out of pollen —
and we ache, not for this or that time, but

for a telling of time without edge
or detail, as when, heat-soaked, we prayed, pushed,

postponed
the bloom's deadline.

THE BODY'S HOPE

I

The world wears coats of bright synthetic skins,
the world wears pelts

with manifest goldleaf, now buttoned up and naped, stub-
raised against the chin, revealing nothing.

As young we were loosed barefoot in our streets,
with flappy undershirts, thin shoulder

straps, and baggy shorts;
the morning rain washed mud-flakes off our knees.

We, only we, were clean.
After we hungered home, we sat on stools, wrapped in thick

towels while we ate — edged in, crooned into cotton.
And Mamá kissed our foreheads,

hand-rubbed our feet, before our clothing.
We were the world again, aware of game apart from game.

~~~

II

Rare-born, garden-bred, they fled embarrassed,
and crouched behind a fire-thorn bush,

each to each shadow with their sun-peel.
The berry clusters swung with tentative flip-flops before

their needy caves, their shy disclosures —
how odd their nakedness, how warlike in the memory

of God come through.
           They whispered back and forth

between hideouts. The man wept,
rough wind between dry lips that carried stormlike:

I loved you once, he said, *grazed you under the vines,
where you templed God, where*

*God incensed our breaths, as a fire would,
at its edges.*

I found you warm and bearing of such spring.
           And she hummed back with hum

of finch whose wings wake
dull at the first chill: *I loved you equally familiar,*

*mindful of the God-groan, God-
hush, God-lent rootings and first thrust after the winter.*

The world wears coats of bright synthetic skins;
the world wears pelts

with manifest goldleaf, unbodied and unable.

~~~

III

Dream back the multi-colored robe,
possess it in the well, in the after-tear of tremors

which unhem full mountain gorges for our cleansing.
                    Reuben, Reuben,

bundle me in the splendor of that coat —
stolen, tucked away,

hence wandered.
The dream wakes wiser in an attic, in spare attires

I have forgotten: why
I wore them, to what dance or to what death,

and for whose watchfulness.
In this lateness, they have become blessed circumstance,

grace-pool I pick through for a finer,
finer gene, native to the naked acre, bare-bone clear.

~~~

IV

Unlike all others, forsaking all others for a night
such as this: we lie, windfall

against windfall, with our wrists inside-out as our truth,
waited, waiting...

There is lace, long-inherited out of a trunk,
with its choice yellow pallor

endemic of age and of kindness.
There is, too, a slim schedule of buttons, like the squares

in a calendar flicked loose to reveal
orant shepherds

or angels. *White, their flux through the room, white,*
the thread of these thoughts and these

sutures preparing my skin
for the sweet intimation; white,

the cloth that must landscape my feet...
All the same, the room sinks into dark wall brocades,

far too dark for a wading of sight
into sight.

And for once, we assume love as body, replenish
god-light with our own,

> *this I'll shade between lips for late giving,*
> *this I'll shelter breathtaken for now.*

Oh, how perfect to confuse groan with grace,
dust with dolor,

the withholding of nothing at all —
not the seed or the soil between limbs — with the largesse

of fields, come to crop, sacramental.

FLORES DE MAYO

Venid y vamos todos con flores a María,
con flores a porfía, que madre nuestra es.
(from a processional hymn)

May in absentia, magenta
in our grip; we cannot give a scent-by-scent

account, born-again children of that long-gone,
long-withered month.

       Pink cellophane hour
of caladium leaves, straw-gold everlastings,

our thin exuding birds of paradise: disquiet
of an orange nib, the wilt and non-

wilt of its pair,
dependent on the day of month,

how sticky or how stupefied our hands.
All in that first forelived desire to be in love —

       Children will always fret in starch,
and we, no less, ran out of chapel

for the *patintero* chalk lines: this,
our tumult, and that yours, border patrols

with arms wide.
Beneath our bursts, ants crawled out in anger.

I stepped on one small mound,
was fired upon a thousand times, poppy-red

around the ankles. Such
is the price of love and of invasion,

price of foreplay.   Don't you see?
              We exercise pursuit again, again,

whether in cotton eyelet, threadwork of old
thread hemming, or tightest thigh-sewn

jeans, clunky shoes or stilettos —
we pray-play for acceptance with eyes borrowing

an old omniscient spring.
              In spite of everything we've

known and tried, how a Beloving lures us;
out of our game, still that darling likelihood...

              Always a summer-rose
              behind the rose-face of a mother.

patintero: children's game in Manila.

DELIRIUM

> *...there is something non-natural or supernatural*
> *about the symptom of "creeping flesh."*
> Rudolf Otto: **The Idea of the Holy**

You came but once
as a non-native secreted in cold, while I was

warm and heart-sore, my *sampaguita* heaped
over the window ledge, Capiz

conch-eyes watching from neat boxes.
You came, a sweet-heart shivering under the blouse,

to take away the thought that this
blessed blessing heat was all away from me.

And feverish I shook.
The afternoon drew glass illusions

on the walls, bold mountain blisters
laureling between the winter domes, my land

of no-seasons awe-struck
before such biting splendor.

What if it were all ice,
December in the tongue as hoarfrost, Eden one

enormous glacier pressing home
and holding? What if

instead of small warm-blooded mammals
coming forth and out of hiding, we came as gaggle

of birds, naturally a-shiver,
pleased, appeased within the rock, where the coves laugh?

                    Mamá would hold me
when the fever rose, the doubt delirious,

damp-cloth the doze,
kiss the eyelids with her thumb, cross-binding.

Mamá, aware of truth and tremor
in the chill that found us.

                    O the flame, white
on the window, upright in the patio, hinges

and door;
the fire that comes too close to worm and dry plum,

next to bed and morning, sleep secure.
                    O the red excess, ripe

thing we crave and burn the heart against,
dread heart unfamiliar.

sampaguita: aromatic Philippine flower.

BELOVED (or: The Legend of Noah's Wife)

Instead of "Is there a God?"
the question becomes: "Will I see God?"
Peter Kreeft: **Love is Stronger than Death**

Through the mildest
or wildest of mornings, through the impossible

autumn come swift, in its switch
from nasturtiums to ice, an old longing lives out

its devotion, always a wife.
In a wrinkle too ripe for her skin, in her aging:

a luminous lurker, a bright absentee, night-
fall zeroed in haste, period-fire her desire cinders into --

Ash to salt-ash, her tastebud implies,
and she washes her lips.

        Where is he whom I've loved incompletely?
The long deck dips undead, blue-wake

under her ribs; the bowsprit points at risk,
while a pigeon sorts weeds on the mopped boards.

Algae-loose, touch-and-go
is her hope in their land-smell and the smell

of a hand who knolled grass at odd hours, knuckled
after the flood just to cradle

her newborns, squeezed
wisely her heart-valve, worn heart, where it flip-

flopped... followed tempest and time-waste,
the red river home,

all its love, all its fishes.
Ah, the inadequate shoremud as platform to pleasure,

the inadequate boulder in blossom.
Inadequate love

for a god slipping westward, clandestine,
all done.

ABSOLUTION

What lifts us out of nightmare is the scent
of well-scrubbed children, loose

molecules out of an old bath's blossoms.
Between six and six-fifteen, the sky would foam

in fuchsias: blush, blush — and we'd rise
to wash our faces.

If others call us now with their night's
mourning we must say: Do not worry; he, too,

will be sweet substance,
lanolin to our touch, cleanliness we wander into,

obsessive
with our washing.

                      Absolve us now, Papá,
inside the oblong of your hands, bones

braced as ours
have been under water: palm

against palm, arms over cold porcelain, chrome
clouds

dripping.
It is the same atonement before meals, before

Holy Orders, before aquatints
with clear flood. Each morning our fingers

dimple out the name: Lavender or
Aloe Vera, or the more exotic Orchid Burst,

shallow now —
A fine skin eases off the bar,

the next skin surfaces a shade whiter for its
temerity, short-lapsed.

And the body comes and comes
again for absolution, regardless of how this

erodes the giver,
drives the face upward, wears it out with new

want — bone-white to the end, until
a ghost emerges sinless.

The Diagnosis

Germ of a clandestine pear tree in the lung:
thus would we describe it, if we

could see the young fruit on the misty
membrane, negligent in growth.

We recognize the kernels in the shed: dry, dark,
ready to flower elsewhere. All

the while, an earnest finger harrows through.
How its prod unnerves us...

And so instead we say: the scanner
has shown a shadow in the right lung.

We will not name it.
                                If only we knew

something about orchards, whether they remain
acres at work through idle moments, or

whether once in a while, in recess,
they become up-down pediments for playful

weeds.
In the market stalls, far removed from locust

haunts, skillet moons announcing rain
(or not), compost heaps coddled

through their decay, there is unerring
unease: the impatience

of plucked figs in cardboard beds, the plums'
aging auras, soft oval sorrows where

they should not be, closebound
to the fruit's navel. We walk through this

limbo with our carts, securing purpose
for this summer or that, this

or that cantaloupe with aromatic nape.
The fruits signify nothing here,

long after they have undressed and the heat
has skated off their backs

into wide baskets.
We weigh them, fondle their necks, drop

them into brown bags
bruising —   all the while,

the pear bruises the lung's harvest.

My Father's House

Threadbare: the curtain we bind,
        waist-high, rib-tight —

meek as Isaac — to allow lattice light
        on our prayer.

Thus we pray back the frailty
        of walls: moth-wing

fever that breaks out in webs
        through the plaster, cracks

the black and white corners, shivers
        rams out of bramble-like

walls.
        Shape, reshape
        the disease, pat the holes
        with soft putty, play pretend.

See the slendering legs near the doorstep,
        thread-bare itch

to get out of the room and its sacrifice.
        Papá this, Papá that...

our return into dangerous
        childhood has lost

its momentum.
        We replaster the room, push

the couch to the sill, where
        a mountainous afghan will

drop lambskin lint, like a morning
                    of flax combing whiteness.

And the walls wrinkle on, skinning
                    homeward, with bone-thin

impatience.
                    There is nothing so strong

as the dying, how securely
                    they settle the house

in its breakage, buff the floors
                    (swish, the shuffle of feet),

bless the chairs with abandon, close
                    the cracks. Ours, those

symptoms of loss and abundance,
                    tales from foregoing gulls —

out of Abraham — flight of lifelines
                    we string and restring,

                    threadbare present.

ONE SWEET INVINCIBLE

An epitaph of purpose, the real thing we know of what we see: broken glass at angles in our ditches, where the run-off becomes all the river we cross, striped cones on the banks where they're building the overpass, cross-dusk of a bridge, new pylons housing a nest of mockingbirds. And if we knew their feathers and their fine beaks for their ends, we would possess them.

Real is the tail-less youngster plopped under the holly to test its truth as one more fledgling; real is the beaver damming its home with our wood, fatter for the bark it peels nightly — wrapped up in its gnawing, so much closer to becoming than our wish to drive it elsewhere.

Your father is going to die. This is a real thing. You know it.

How the broken glass ceases to be pitcher or scent flask, or a little girl's moonlike mirror in her hand, how the nest husks into summer, shelled by the screech of the backhoe, how the creature flees death for a while, how the trapper visits the pond with his license, to finish our preference.

Reality is that which needs nothing at all but its aim to be real, the unfellable thing we have loved in the felled trees where the paving goes on, in a childhood we lived through a handful of mirrors, in the rickety blossom of bird flopping in, out of balance. Now we want it as eggshell in hand, fragile oval fulfilling our fist at the side of his bed. Now we exchange it for the pressure he'll yield any moment, set to flight

(sweet invincible thing) on his cheeks.

Nunc Dimitis (or: A Viable Good-bye)

Identical, our daily movements into sleep:
      the bed-lamp swiveled off, sigh

of shoulders idling into place; we hollow
      out a cave for the left hip, and the left

hand slips under the pillow with its beads,
      dangerously tight.

We've done this all our lives,
      since Papá crossed our foreheads

with his thumb, pulling the sheets
      over our shoulders.

Other things change: we do not drop
      raw egg into our soup, or boil sweet

onions; we walk barefoot despite
      Mamá's clear intonation (you must

wear your *chinelas* in the house), and
      some time between three and four,

we disengage a rosary.
      Our days are pure and plentiful —

Hawks in a backyard roost, a starling
      arcs under makeshift protection;

a single-lily pond, a single goldfish
      raises the ripples, lip over lip

until the coming ice;
      we pluck, pull, repossess: this word

for that loquacious life; that word
      for an entangled ours.

The neighbor's foxglove spring, the next-
      door gutter pouring out its rain,

the singular procession trickling by,
      with its own widower —

Once more, we open up the linen, peel
      after peel, unroll

the blackstone litany:
      Through them, with them, in them.

So little have we done to call our own,
      so little.